Life in ANCIENT TIMES

How The
AZTECS
Lived

Anita Ganeri

Gareth Stevens
Publishing

Please visit our Web site, www.garethstevens.com. For a free color catalog of all our high-quality books, call toll free 1-800-542-2595 or fax 1-877-542-2596.

Library of Congress Cataloging-in-Publication Data

Ganeri, Anita, 1961-
How the Aztecs lived / Anita Ganeri.
    p. cm. — (Life in ancient times)
Includes index.
ISBN 978-1-4339-4097-2 (library binding)
I. Aztecs—Social life and customs—Juvenile literature. 2. Aztecs—History—Juvenile literature.
I. Title.
F1219.76.S64G36 2011
972—dc22

J972
GAN

2010015865

This edition first published in 2011 by
Gareth Stevens Publishing
111 East 14th Street, Suite 349
New York, NY 10003

Copyright © 2011 Wayland/Gareth Stevens Publishing

Editorial Director: Kerri O'Donnell
Art Director: Haley Harasymiw

Photo Credits:
AKG London Ltd: 9 (Franz Hogenbery), 22 (Erich Lessing), 28; The Bridgeman Art Library *cover* and 1 (Biblioteca Nazionale Centrale, Florence, Italy); CM Dixon: 15; ET Archive: 8, 13, 17, 20, 21, 32, 25; South American Pictures 5, 7, 12 (all by Tony Morrison); Tony Stone Images: 4 (Robert Frerch); Werner Forman Archive: 11, 14, 18, 19, 24, 26, 27, 29.

Printed in the China

CPSIA compliance information: Batch #WAS10GS: For further information contact Gareth Stevens, New York, New York at 1-800-542-2595.

CONTENTS

WHO WERE THE AZTECS?

The Aztecs were a warlike people who began living in the country we now call Mexico about 800 years ago. At first, they wandered from place to place. Later, they settled down in one place and built a village. Within 100 years, the village had grown into a great city called Tenochtitlan (pronounced "tay-notch-teet-lahn").

▼ Part of Mexico near the modern city of Veracruz. This was one of the many areas ruled by the Aztecs.

▲ The Aztecs invented their own calendar. This stone is a calendar stone. It shows the Aztec sun god in the center. Around him are signs for the days of the week.

Although the Aztecs were fierce warriors, They were also skilled in writing, building, arts, and crafts. They used picture writing for keeping records and writing about their religion and history. They built towering temples to worship their gods. Aztec craftworkers made beautiful jewelry and pottery.

THE AZTEC EMPIRE

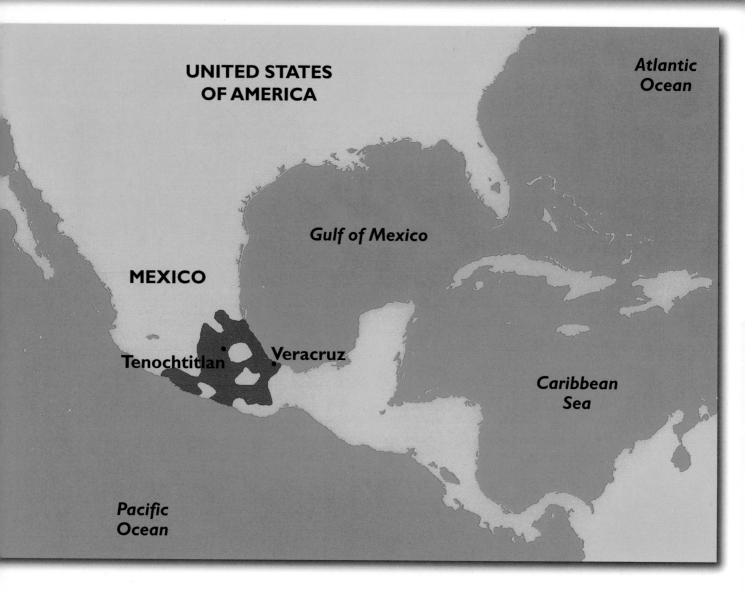

UNITED STATES
OF AMERICA

Atlantic
Ocean

Gulf of Mexico

MEXICO

Tenochtitlan · ·Veracruz

Caribbean
Sea

Pacific
Ocean

▲ At its greatest size, the Aztec empire covered all the lands shown shaded in red on the map above.

At the height of its power, the Aztec empire reached all the way across Mexico from the east to the west coast. It contained hundreds of towns and cities, with over 15 million people. Tenochtitlan was the largest city in the empire.

Most of the people in the empire were not Aztecs. They belonged to other groups, or tribes, who were conquered by the Aztec army. They had to pay a tribute or tax to the Aztec emperor. They did not have money so they paid with valuable goods, such as gold, precious stones, and exotic feathers. If they could not pay, they were punished.

▼ You can still see the ruins of Tenochtitlan if you visit Mexico City today. The new city was built over the old one. This picture shows part of the Great Temple.

7

CAPITAL CITY

The capital city of the Aztec empire was Tenochtitlan. It was built in the middle of a swampy lake called Lake Texcoco. A story tells how the Aztecs built the city at the spot where an eagle was perched on top of a prickly cactus plant. This was the sign that the sun god had told them to look for.

Tenochtitlan was a busy, bustling city, with about 200,000 people. In the city center stood the sacred square with its great temples and grand palaces. Instead of streets, the city was crisscrossed by canals. Most people traveled around in canoes.

▼ This painting shows an eagle perched on top of a cactus. The name Tenochtitlan means "beside cactus rock."

▼ This picture shows how the city of Tenochtitlan was divided into four quarters. These were called the Place of the Mosquitoes, the Place of the Gods, the Place of Flowers, and the Place of the Herons.

MEXICO, REGIA ET CELEBRIS HISPANIÆ NO: VAE CIVITAS

Cum Priuilegio.

Aztec society was divided into four groups. The nobles helped the emperor to rule the empire. They were wealthy and powerful. Most Aztecs were commoners. They lived by farming small plots of land. Serfs worked on land owned by the nobles. The last group were the slaves. They were often prisoners of war.

▶ On special occasions, the emperor was carried through the city on a throne. Ordinary people had to look down as he passed. They were not allowed to look at him.

THE GREAT SPEAKER

The emperor was called the Great Speaker. He was head of the government and army. His deputy was an official called the Snake Woman, even though this was a man. The last Great Speaker was Montezuma II. He ruled from 1502 to 1520. His name is usually written as "Montezuma."

▲ This beautiful shield belonged to one of the Aztec emperors. It is made of brightly colored feathers from tropical birds.

The ruler of the Aztecs was called the emperor. He was the most important Aztec of all. The emperor was treated like a god. Only the nobles and the high priests were allowed to talk to him. He lived in a magnificent palace in the center of Tenochtitlan.

11

AZTEC HOMES AND FARMS

Aztec farmers grew corn, vegetables, fruit, and flowers on plots of land called chinampas. These were like small islands in the lake. They were built from reeds and branches, covered in thick, black mud scooped up from the lake bottom. A strong willow fence stopped the mud from being washed away.

Ordinary Aztecs lived in simple mud-brick huts with roofs of thatched straw or reeds. Inside, people sat on the floor on low stools or mats. They slept on mats spread out on the floor. They had very little furniture.

▲ The chinampas tended by Aztec farmer looked very much like the ones in the picture above. They were used because there was no farmland in the city.

▼ The most important part of an Aztec home was the hearth. Here, the family cooked their food over a fire.

FAMILY LIFE

▼ Pottery bowls like these were used in Aztec houses. They were made and decorated by women.

Family life was very important to the Aztecs. The father was the head of the family. It was his job to work hard to look after his wife and children. His wife looked after the home.

AZTEC SCHOOLS

The Aztecs were one of the few ancient civilizations to allow both boys and girls to go to school. Boys from poorer families went to a military school to learn how to become soldiers. Some girls from poorer families went to schools where they learned to sing and dance.

Aztec children were strictly brought up. They had to obey their parents at all times, without complaining. Naughty children were harshly punished. They might be tied up and left outside all night, or pricked with sharp cactus spines!

From the age of seven, many Aztec boys from wealthy families went to school to study history and religion. They also learned how to use weapons and fight. Most girls stayed at home. Their mothers taught them how to cook, do the housework, and weave clothes and blankets.

▲ Aztec children had toys, just like modern children. This child's rattle was made in the shape of a woman holding a child.

15

Aztecs could tell how important or wealthy people were by looking at their clothes. Ordinary people wore plain clothes made from cactus fibers. Only nobles were allowed to wear clothes of fine cotton and long, flowing cloaks. On their feet, rich people wore sandals. Poorer people went barefoot.

◄ Aztec women wore brightly colored headdresses and shawls that they made themselves. Ordinary men wore plain tunics.

▼ Some warriors wore special clothing as a reward for bravery. The best warriors were the Jaguars and Eagles. They dressed in jaguar skins and eagle feathers.

The Aztecs made beautiful jewelry from gold and precious stones. It was very costly and only wealthy people could afford it. Only the emperor and nobles were allowed to wear feather headdresses, or turquoise jewelry. It was a serious crime to wear clothes belonging to a richer group.

FOOD AND DRINK

The Aztecs' main food was corn (maize). This was ground into flour and used to make round, flat pancakes called tortillas. People used these to scoop up other foods or wrapped them around meat or vegetables. The Aztecs liked spicy food and many dishes were flavored with hot chili peppers.

▲ A local market in Mexico. On sale are tomatoes, spicy chilies, and other vegetables that would have been seen in an Aztec market.

Hot chocolate was a favorite drink. It was made from the beans of the cacao tree. They were crushed, boiled with water, and flavored with vanilla or honey. But chocolate was so expensive that only rich people could afford to have it often. Ordinary people mostly drank water or strong cactus beer, called *pulqué*.

▼ This hare-shaped cup was used in a wealthy home for drinking chocolate. The chocolate was drunk through golden straws.

AN AZTEC MEAL

To eat like an Aztec, buy some tortillas from the supermarket. Ask an adult to fry some thin strips of chicken. Wrap some in a tortilla with some spicy beans and chopped tomato. Add a spoonful of guacamole (a paste made from avocados) and eat!

GODS AND TEMPLES

Religion was very important to the Aztecs. They worshiped many gods and goddesses. The main gods were Centeotl, god of the corn, Tlaloc, god of rain, Huitzilopochtli, god of war, and Tonatiuh, god of the sun. The Aztecs held special ceremonies to please the gods. They believed that if they didn't, the gods would punish them.

▼ This picture shows a human sacrifice. The priest offers the victim's heart and blood to the sun, to keep the sun alive.

The biggest buildings in an Aztec city were the temples built to the gods. A shrine stood on top of a tall, stepped pyramid. Every day, at the Great Temple in Tenochtitlan, people were led up the steps to be killed as a gift to the god of the sun. It was thought to be a great honor to die in this way.

▲ A mask showing the god Quetzalcoatl. He was the god of learning and the wind.

▲ Players had to hit the ball through a stone ring like this one, placed high up on a wall at an awkward angle. It wasn't easy to score a goal!

Sports and games were played as part of Aztec religious ceremonies. The most important was the sacred game of tlachtli. It was played on a special stone court near the Great Temple.

Tlachtli was a sport a little like basketball. Two teams of players tried to hit a rubber ball through a stone ring. But they could not use their hands or feet, only their hips, elbows, and knees.

SACRED GAME

Tlachtli was more than a game. It had a religious meaning. The ballcourt was like the world, and the ball like the moon and sun. Not only did the losing team have to give up all their possessions, but they also risked being sacrificed to the gods.

Another popular Aztec game was called patolli. This was a board game a little like backgammon. Players used dried beans as dice and colored stones as counters. They threw the beans and moved their counters across the board.

▲ Playing patolli was a very popular pastime. The board was divided into 52 parts like the Aztec century.

WAR AND WARRIORS

From an early age, Aztec boys were sent to special schools called telpochcalli to train as soldiers. Here, they learned how to fight bravely and to handle weapons such as bows and arrows, clubs, and spears. For protection, they wore padded armor and carried shields. Then they were ready to go to war.

▼ This painting shows two Aztec war chiefs. The Aztec army was very powerful. It conquered new lands and kept the empire under control.

Every boy dreamed of becoming a great warrior. He was made a full warrior when he had taken three prisoners of war. The best warriors were rewarded with land, titles, and important jobs.

▼ The head of an Eagle warrior, one of the best and bravest Aztec warriors of all. To become an Eagle, you had to take many prisoners in battle.

TRADE AND MARKETS

Aztec merchants were called pochteca. They traveled all over the empire to bring back exotic goods. These included cacao beans, jaguar skins, and feathers from tropical birds. Some merchants also worked as spies for the emperor. They brought information about any signs of trouble in the empire.

▼ The picture below shows Lord Nose, the god of merchants.

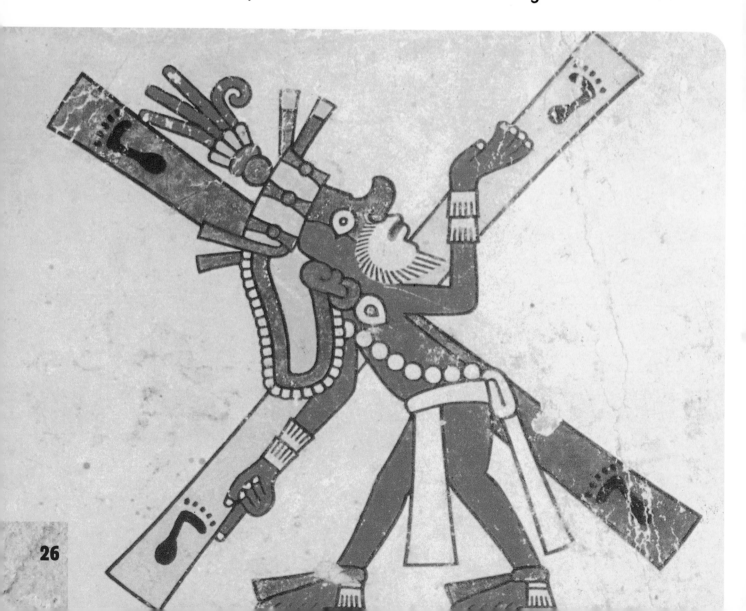

▲ This is what the market place at Tenochtitlan might have looked like. It was a lively, colorful place full of noise and bustle.

The merchants' goods were bought and sold at market. The Aztecs did not pay with money. They paid for goods with other goods. Market inspectors checked that the merchants charged a fair price.

THE END OF THE EMPIRE

In 1521, the Aztec empire was brought to an end by Spanish invaders. They were led by a man named Hernando Cortés. The Spanish had heard about the Aztecs' gold and were determined to steal it.

Cortés and his men arrived in Mexico in 1519 and marched to Tenochtitlan. They were amazed by the city's splendor. At first, the Aztecs thought they were friends. But Cortés seized the city and took the emperor, Montezuma II, prisoner. Montezuma was later killed and Aztec rule ended.

▼ At first, the Aztecs welcomed Cortes and treated him like a god. Here, they are giving him a necklace as a gift.

▶ A golden pendant of a god. The Spanish stole huge amounts of Aztec gold for themselves.

HOW DO WE KNOW?

The Spanish destroyed many Aztec buildings and temples. They built their own cities and churches in their place. But archaeologists have found some Aztec ruins, like those of the Great Temple in Mexico City. They have also discovered statues, pottery, and jewelry, which help to tell us about life in Aztec times.

IMPORTANT DATES

600 The Aztecs believed that their god, Quetzalcoatl, died in this year.

ca. 1111 The Mexica people leave Aztlan in search of a new home.

ca. 1200 The Aztecs settle in the Valley of Mexico after wandering for many years.

1325 The Aztecs build the city of Tenochtitlan in the middle of swampy Lake Texcoco.

1367–1395 Rule of Acamapichtli.

1396–1417 Rule of Huitzilihuitl. Early 1400s Tenochtitlan becomes a powerful city that controls the lands around it.

1417–1427 Rule of Chimalpopoca.

1427–1440 Rule of Itzcoatl.

1440–1469 Rule of Montezuma I. The Aztecs conquer new lands and the empire grows in size to become very important.

1460 20,000 people are sacrificed at a big religious ceremony.

1469–1481 Rule of Axayacatl.

1470 The Aztecs try to conquer both the Mixtecs and the Zapotecs but fail to do so.

1473 The Aztecs conquer the city of Tlatelolco.

1481–1486 Rule of Tizoc. He built the Great Temple in Tenochtitlan.

1486–1502 Rule of Ahuitzotl.

1500 Tenochtitlan is flooded.

1502–1520 Rule of Montezuma II. The Aztec empire is at the height of its power. The Aztecs rule over 10 million people.

1504 The Spanish leader, Hernando Cortés, leaves Spain on his journey to find gold.

1511 The Spanish arrive in Cuba.

1517 The first Spanish expedition to Mexico takes place.

1519 The Spanish leader, Hernando Cortés, lands on the east coast of Mexico. He marches inland to Tenochtitlan. At first, the emperor welcomes him warmly because he thinks he is the god Quetzalcoatl.

1520 Montezuma II is killed.

1521 The Spanish attack and capture Tenochtitlan. Aztec rule comes to an end between April 28 and August 13.

GLOSSARY

Archaeologists People who study the past.

Canal A long stretch of water that boats can travel along.

Chili peppers Small, hot peppers for flavoring food.

Chinampas Mud islands in Lake Texcoco on which farmers grew crops.

Codex An Aztec book that was folded like an accordion, in a zigzag.

Commoners People who do not come from noble families.

Deputy An important official who is second in command to someone.

Empire A group of countries or lands ruled over by an emperor.

Exotic Unusual and precious.

Nobles People who come from powerful families.

Pochteca An Aztec merchant.

Quetzal A brightly colored tropical bird.

Sacrifice An offering made to the gods.

Serf Slaves who were sold as part of the land that they worked on.

Taxes Money that people pay to their rulers.

Telpochcalli A training school for Aztec warriors.

Temple A building where people worship gods or goddesses.

Tortillas Round pancakes made of ground corn.

Tribute A type of tax paid to the Aztec emperor by the people he had conquered. It was paid in goods, not money.

Turquoise A type of precious blue stone.

FURTHER READING AND WEB SITES

Books

The Aztecs
by Anita Ganeri
Compass Point Books, 2007

The Aztecs: Life in Tenochtitlan
by Matt Doeden
Millbrook Press, 2009

How to be an Aztec Warrior
by Fiona MacDonald
National Geographic Children's Books, 2008

Web Sites

http://library.thinkquest.org/27981/?tqskip=1

http://www.aztecs.mrdonn.org/

INDEX